WILLY WOO'S feeling ANGRY

Ari Huffines

Illustrated by 18/1 Graphics Studio

*To mine and your children,
whose laughter teaches us
to live lightly, love deeply,
and embrace the wonder of play.*

Hi!
Nice to meet you.
My name is Willy Woo.

I've got lots of feelings—
Yes, more than a few!

Sometimes I feel happy.
Sometimes I feel blue.

But sometimes I'm angry—
It bursts right through!

I go to my friend's
For a fun little play,

With my speedy
red race car
To brighten the day.

I **zoom** the car forward,
And zip it right back.

Laughing and racing
Along the big track.

But then my
friend asks me,
"Can I have a go?"

He grabs my red car
And he puts on a show.

He **zips** it around,
And he makes a sharp spin.
Then tosses it high
With a mischievous grin.

It flies through the air,

Then goes CRASH!! on the floor.
He's broken my car!
This is hard to ignore.

Now I feel ANGRY—
It's easy to see,
A fire inside
Rising in me.

I feel the
red heat
Starting down
in my feet,

Rising up
through
my chest,
And the fire
won't retreat.

My body gets **HOT.**
My fists get **TIGHT.**

I feel **POWERFUL,**
And I'm **ready to FIGHT.**

Then rage comes in,

And it strikes just like that.
It's like a volcano Under my hat.

I want to **shout.**
I want to **roar.**
I want to **stomp**
across the floor.

My **anger** is loud,
Boiling up with a fizz,
But I'm still in charge—
I'm the boss of this bizz.

You see,
there's a trick,
And it might
help you too.

I STOP...
I NOTICE...
And I think
what to do.

I say, "I feel **ANGRY**,
And, hey, it's okay.

It's not scary,
Just how I'm feeling today."

Sometimes our anger
Just wants to protect,

When something feels
Wrong or incorrect.

It's like my body
Is shouting out, **"HEY!"**
But I still choose
What I do or say.

I breathe big and slow.

I count:

In and out, let it go,
Till the fire is less than before.

Already, I feel **calmer**.
Breathing works
like a fire truck,

Cooling me down,
When I'm feeling
quite stuck.

So if you feel **angry,**
Like I sometimes do,
Just take a **deep breath**
And talk it through.

START
IMPULSE TO YELL AND BITE
IMPULSE TO HIT AND GRAB
IMPULSE TO KICK AND STOMP